Hiring Staff

By Daniel Barnett

The Employment Law Library

All books in the Employment Law Library are sent for free to members of the HR Inner Circle.

1. Employee Investigations
2. GDPR for HR Professionals
3. Preventing and Defending Employee Stress Claims
4. Employment Tribunal Time Limits
5. Deconstructing TUPE
6. Changing Terms & Conditions
7. Constructive Dismissal
8. Resolving Grievances
9. HR Hazards
10. Employment Status
11. Spotting Malingering
12. Employment Tribunal Compensation
13. Hiring Staff
14. Computer and Social Media Misuse

Published by Employment Law Services Limited, Unit 3, Chequers Farm, Chequers Lane, Watford, Hertfordshire WD25 0LG

ISBN 978-1-913925-07-9

EMPLOYMENT
LAW
MATTERS

Acknowledgments

This is the thirteenth book in my series of mini guides on employment law for HR professionals.

Discrimination law touches on every stage of the recruitment journey, including designing the advertisement and person specification, shortlisting, testing and interviewing, interpreting references and, potentially, drafting the contents of the offer and contract of employment.

Data protection law impinges upon every part of the journey that results in the gathering and processing of personal data, including the advertisement stage, where a statement pointing to the employer's data protection policy and privacy notice should be made.

On top of this are the complex laws and rules relating to the right to work in the UK, and a failure to adhere to these laws can result in severe penalties. Added to this is the spent convictions legislation and the obligations in relation to what information needs to be given to a new employee or worker.

As always, there are a number of people to thank. First and foremost, I'd like to thank David Appleton for his help with the content, and Mike Clyne for contributing a chapter. I'd also like to thank Tincuta Moscaliuc for the layout and design, Aaron Gaff for proofreading and Maria Rodriguez for converting the book into the formats needed for Amazon.

I'd also like to thank the members of the HR Inner Circle for whom I primarily write these small books (and who get them all for free as part of their membership). If you're interested in learning more about HR Inner Circle membership (www.hrinnercircle.co.uk), there is more information at the back of this book.

Daniel Barnett
August 2022

**THE UK'S LEADING
YOUTUBE CHANNEL FOR
LAW EXPLAINER VIDEOS**

WWW.YOUTUBELEGAL.CO.UK

ABOUT THE AUTHOR

 Daniel Barnett is a leading employment law barrister practising from Outer Temple Chambers. With 25 years' experience defending public and private sector employers against employment claims, he has represented a Royal Family, several international airlines, FTSE-100 companies and various NHS Trusts and local authorities. Employee clients include David & Victoria Beckham's nanny and Paul Mason (subject of the ITV documentary 'Britain's Fattest Man').

Daniel is a past chair of the Employment Lawyers' Association's publishing committee and electronic services working party. He is the author or co-author of eight books, including the Law Society Handbook on Employment Law (currently in its 8th edition). He is the creator of the Employment Law (UK) mailing list, an email alerter bulletin service sending details of breaking news in employment law three times a week to 33,000 recipients.

Legal directories describe him as 'extremely knowledgeable and [he] can absorb pages of instructions at lightning speed', 'involved in a number of highly contentious matters', 'singled out for his work for large blue-chip companies', 'combination of in-depth legal knowledge, pragmatism, quick response times and approachability', 'inexhaustible', 'tenacious', 'knowledgeable', and 'an excellent advocate'.

He is one of the leading speakers and trainers on the employment law and HR circuit. He has presented seminars for the House of Commons, the BBC, Oxford University, HSBC, Barclays Bank, Ocado, and dozens of other organisations in-house. In 2013, 2014, 2016, and 2019 he designed — and was the sole speaker at — the Employment Law MasterClass national tour.

As well as full-time practice as a barrister and speaker, Daniel is the founder of the HR Inner Circle – a membership club for smart, ambitious HR Professionals. In 2007, he co-founded CPD Webinars Ltd, then the UK's leading webinar training company for lawyers, and sold it to Thomson Reuters in 2011.

Daniel is widely sought after as a commentator in both broadcast and print media on all legal issues. Since 2010 he has presented the Legal Hour on LBC Radio. In 2019, he launched Employment Law Matters, a weekly podcast with short explanations of employment law topics. Subscribe at www.danielbarnett.co.uk/podcast

www.danielbarnett.co.uk
Temple, London

JOIN DANIEL EVERY SATURDAY EVENING
AT 9PM WHEN HE PRESENTS THE

LBC LEGAL HOUR

— OR CATCH UP VIA THE GLOBAL PLAYER,
AT bit.ly/lbclegalhour

SATURDAYS, 9PM

Contents

1. Introduction   13

2. Employee, worker, agency worker
or independent contractor?   15

3. Discrimination   19

4. Data protection   43

5. The advertisement and job description   57

6. Sifting the applications and shortlisting   67

7. Interview(s) and the
decision-making process   71

8. The right to work in the United Kingdom   75

9. The offer of employment   81

10. Pre-employment screening   83

11. Seeking references   89

12. Police checks and criminal records   95

13. The contract of employment   103

Chapter 1
Introduction

The Institute for Employment Studies' latest available Labour Market Statistics (for May 2022) indicate that there are over 1.3 million unfilled vacancies in the UK; a figure over double that from a year ago, and 50% higher than pre-pandemic. The number of unemployed people per vacancy is at its lowest for at least half a century. Those figures indicate a significant amount of recruitment activity, with many businesses chasing fewer candidates and having to resort to tactics such as significantly raising starting salaries and offering other incentives.

Despite the stresses that this dynamic causes, the hiring of new staff can be an exciting adventure for a business. Whether you are increasing your workforce or replacing someone, a new hire is the result of an investment that you will want to maximise. Alongside effective management, the recruitment process is probably the most important part of the journey that a business undertakes with its staff members. Getting it right at the start will make a huge difference to the way the journey progresses.

This latest volume in the series of legal guides for HR Professionals examines the full range of employment law issues arising from the hiring of staff. It covers the issue of deciding whether to hire employees, agency staff or self-employed contractors; discrimination and data protection law in general; the wording of advertisements and the drafting of job descriptions; shortlisting and the interview process; the taking up of references; criminal checks; the drafting of the offer letter; and the contents of the contract of employment.

If you know that you want to recruit an employee (as opposed to engaging an agency worker or independent contractor) you can skip Chapter 2, save for checking out the list of employee's rights if you would find that useful. However, I recommend that you read Chapter 3 and Chapter 4 in their entirety, as they set out the key elements of discrimination and data protection law, both of which pervade the whole of the recruitment process to a greater or lesser degree.

This publication is aimed at private employers, and it does not cover recruitment agents or the additional duties of public bodies.

Chapter 2

Employee, worker, agency worker or independent contractor?

Book 10 of the Employment Law Library offers a detailed look at Employment Status. In it, I examine the differences between an employee, a worker, an agency worker and an independent contractor, among other types of relationships, including the different legal rights that each has.

While there is a huge difference in legal terms between an employee, a worker, an agency worker and an independent contractor, often there is no discernible difference from an outsider's viewpoint, as they may all be doing exactly the same job. Your customers and clients may not have a clue about the employment status of the person they interact with and, in many cases, they do not need to know. However, from a cost and compliance point of view, the status of the person you hire to do a particular job is important.

How to decide which type of hire to make

There are no hard and fast rules but, in general terms, if you are looking for a long-term hire, someone who you will want to invest in, or someone senior, you should probably recruit an employee. You may wish to enrol them in one or more incentive schemes and make a range of benefits and training opportunities available to them so as to incentivise them and nurture their loyalty and long-term commitment.

Agency workers or the self-employed may be more suitable when you only require someone for the short term or a specific project, whom you will not wish to promote or train, and who will not have managerial responsibilities. Beware, though, not to engage a self-employed person in a way that is more akin to employment, as the Employment Tribunal (ET) and/ or HMRC can make a finding that a relationship is an employment one regardless of how it the parties label it.

Fixed-term employment contracts have been on the rise, according to the Labour Market Statistics published by the Institute for Employment Studies (May 2021). This trend may be because such contracts give employees flexibility and certainty, and they are particularly helpful where the need for the particular work or task is of limited duration or where temporary cover is needed for a permanent staff member on maternity leave.

A fixed-term employment contract is an alternative to engaging a temporary agency or other worker. Remember, though, that the expiry of a fixed-term contract may constitute a dismissal for redundancy pay and unfair dismissal purposes (both of which normally require two years' employment) and that fixed-term employees are entitled to the same contractual benefits and facilities as permanent staff, under the Fixed-term Employees (Prevention of Less Favourable Treatment) Regulations 2002 (although not all kinds of contracts that may be called 'fixed term' fall within the provisions of these regulations).

Of course, other types of employment arrangements are possible, such as casual employees, zero-hours contracts, job sharing arrangements and/or part-time work. Remember that zero-hours contracts (which may not necessarily be employment contracts) cannot contain an exclusivity clause requiring the worker to work exclusively for the business. In addition, part-time staff are protected against less favourable treatment by the Part-Time Workers (Prevention of Less Favourable Treatment) Regulations 2000.

Chapter 3
Discrimination

The recruitment process does not create any unfair dismissal risks unless an unusual automatic unfair dismissal situation arises shortly after a new employee commences work. However, the risk of a discrimination claim does rear its head at various stages of recruitment. Especially risky are:

- the wording of the advertisement

- the wording of the job description or specification and role requirements

- the shortlisting stage

- the interviews

The tangible risk is that a business is sued by an unsuccessful candidate for unlawful discrimination in its recruitment process or, potentially worse, that it attracts the attention of the Equality and Human Rights Commission (EHRC). I examine the specifics of such claims in more detail in subsequent chapters but, briefly, a business that unlawfully discriminates could face:

- a finding by an employment tribunal (ET) that the business has discriminated against a claimant

- an order by an ET that the business must pay the claimant compensation for any financial losses, as well as for injury to feelings, personal injury and/or aggravated damages

- a recommendation by an ET as to the steps the business should take to reduce the adverse effects of discrimination

- an investigation by the EHRC

- the serving of a notice by the EHRC recommending action or requiring the business to prepare an action plan

- having to enter into a binding agreement with the EHRC not to commit an unlawful act, or to take positive steps to that end

- an injunction sought by the EHRC in the County Court

Whichever occurs, it is an unwelcome distraction for the business, and it could have a significant impact financially, reputationally and in terms of management time swallowed up.

In order to mitigate against the risk, you need to understand the basic elements of discrimination law. The key piece of legislation is the Equality Act 2010, and the starting point in understanding discrimination law is the 'protected characteristics'. These arc the inherent characteristics of a person that may be the cause of them suffering unlawful discrimination. The protected characteristics are:

- sex

- marital or civil partnership status

- race

- gender reassignment

- religion or belief

- sexual orientation

- pregnancy or maternity leave

- age

- disability

Let's look at these characteristics in a little more detail.

Sex specifically refers to a male or a female of any age. A comparator for the purposes of showing sex discrimination is someone of the opposite sex (see below under 'direct discrimination' for an explanation of 'comparator'). Sex for these purposes does not include reassigned or preferred genders, or sexual orientation.

Marital or civil partnership status refers to someone whose marriage is legally recognised in the UK and someone whose civil partnership is registered under the Civil Partnership Act 2004. The status of being unmarried or single is not protected, even if the person was once married or in a civil partnership. An intention to marry or enter into a civil partnership also does not confer any protection.

Race is defined as including colour, nationality and ethnic or national origins. A racial group will share colour, nationality and/or ethnic or national origins (such as British people, Black British people, or South Asians) and can also be made up of more than one racial group. Nationality refers to the legal relationship between a person and a state through birth or naturalisation, while national origins must have identifiable elements, both historic and geographic. For example, the Scottish have a separate national origin to the English.

Ethnic origin refers to an ethnic group defined by the courts. The ethnic group must regard itself and be regarded by others as a distinct and separate community because of certain characteristics, including a long-shared history and a cultural tradition of its own. A common language, literature, religion and/or geographical origin, among other things, can also be present. Sikhs, Jews, Roma, Irish Travellers, Scottish Gypsies and Scottish Travellers have all been confirmed by the courts to be ethnic groups capable of protection.

Gender reassignment refers to people who are proposing to undergo, are undergoing or have undergone a process (or part of a process) to reassign their sex by changing physiological or other attributes of sex. It is not necessary for someone to undergo a medical process to be protected, and someone who starts the process but stops partway through is also protected. Someone who 'cross-dresses' for reasons of gender identity is also protected.

Religion or belief includes any religion and religious or philosophical belief, as well as a lack of such religion or belief. To count as a protected religion, it must have a clear structure and belief system. Sects or denominations within a religion may count as a religion under the Equality Act 2010.

A belief must affect how a person lives their life, and must:

- be genuinely held

- not merely be an opinion based on the state of information available

- be a weighty and substantial aspect of human life and behaviour

- attain a certain level of cogency, seriousness, cohesion and importance

- be worthy of respect in a democratic society, not be incompatible with human dignity and not conflict with the fundamental rights of others

Humanism, atheism and ethical veganism have been found to count as protectable philosophical beliefs.

Sexual orientation refers to a person's sexual orientation towards persons of the same sex, the opposite sex or either sex. People can be protected in relation to their appearance, the places they visit and the people they associate with.

Regarding **pregnancy or maternity**, the Equality Act 2010 protects a woman from being treated unfavourably because of her pregnancy or related illness, or because she is exercising, has exercised or has sought to exercise her right to maternity leave. The protection lasts from the date when the woman becomes pregnant until she returns to work or the end of her maternity leave period, whichever is earlier. Outside of that protected period, unfavourable treatment because of her pregnancy would be discrimination because of sex.

Age is defined by reference to a person's age group, which can mean people of the same age or range of ages. They can be wide ('under 50') or narrow ('people born in 2000'), and the meaning can differ depending on the context. A comparator could be someone from any other age group.

Disability is defined in the Equality Act 2010 by reference to a disabled person:

> "A person (P) has a disability if—
>
> - P has a physical or mental impairment, and
>
> - the impairment has a substantial and long-term adverse effect on P's ability to carry out normal day-to-day activities."

'Long term' in this definition means that the impairment has lasted, or is likely to last, for at least 12 months or for the rest of the person's life. People who used to have a disability under this definition continue to be protected after the disability has ceased. Cancer, HIV infection and multiple sclerosis are deemed disabilities from the point of diagnosis, as are progressive conditions which get worse over time in certain circumstances.

Types of discrimination

Let's turn now to what sorts of conduct may constitute unlawful discrimination. There are four main types identified in the Equality Act 2010:

- direct discrimination

- indirect discrimination

- victimisation

- harassment

Direct discrimination, which is essentially less favourable treatment because of a protected characteristic, is defined in section 13(1) of the Equality Act 2010:

> *"A person (A) discriminates against another (B) if, because of a protected characteristic, A treats B less favourably than A treats or would treat others."*

'Less favourable treatment' is an important concept, and it is aimed at ensuring that a person with a particular protected characteristic is treated equally compared to others who do not have that protected characteristic. This concept has sparked a significant amount of case law, much of it about identifying who the appropriate 'comparator' is.

In other words, someone (let's call her Mildred) complaining of direct discrimination must show that they have been treated less favourably than an actual individual or a hypothetical person, in both cases because of Mildred's protected characteristic. Obviously, there should be no material differences between Mildred's circumstances and those of the actual or hypothetical comparator, although it is not appropriate to imagine a comparator who is an exact clone of Mildred, save for the protected characteristic, as you often cannot separate a person's circumstances from their characteristic.

Different protected characteristics will require a focus on different aspects of a person. For example, in the case of direct disability discrimination, the abilities of the disabled person and the comparator must not be materially different, whereas, in a case of sexual orientation direct discrimination, the fact that one person is married to a person of the same sex and the comparator is married to some of the opposite sex is not treated as a material difference.

Positive discrimination (referred to as 'positive action' in the Equality Act 2010) is a type of direct discrimination, and it is not allowed, except where the purpose is to correct the effect of a pre-existing discriminatory disadvantage being suffered by a group of people.

Section 159 of the Equality Act 2010 deals specifically with positive action in recruitment. It applies if you reasonably think that:

> (a) persons who share a protected characteristic suffer a disadvantage connected to the characteristic

> (b) participation in an activity by persons who share a protected characteristic is disproportionately low

Where this is the case, you are allowed to take specified action with the aim of enabling or encouraging persons who share the protected characteristic to overcome or minimise that disadvantage or participate in that activity. That specified action is:

> *"treating a person (A) more favourably in connection with recruitment or promotion than another person (B) because A has the protected characteristic but B does not."*

Positive action is only allowed, though, where three conditions are met. Using the same labels of A and B, the conditions are that:

1. A is as qualified as B to be recruited.

2. you do not have a policy of treating persons who share the protected characteristic more favourably in connection with recruitment or promotion than persons who do not share it.

3. taking the positive action is "a proportionate means of achieving the aim of overcoming or minimising the disadvantage or participating in the activity.

You are allowed to (and, sometimes, must) treat a disabled person *more* favourably than a non-disabled person. For example, an advertisement may specifically seek people who are disabled or target disabled people by advertising in media primarily read by disabled persons, such as publications for the visually impaired.

Indirect discrimination

Indirect discrimination occurs when a person (let's call him Manfred) applies to another person (we'll call her Mildred) a provision, criterion or practice (PCP) which is discriminatory in relation to a relevant protected characteristic that Mildred has (such as her age, sex, disability or religion).

A PCP is discriminatory if:

- Manfred also applies it to persons with whom Mildred does not share the characteristic

- the PCP puts persons with whom Mildred shares the characteristic at a particular disadvantage when compared with persons with whom she does not share it

- it causes or would cause Mildred to suffer that disadvantage

- Manfred cannot show the PCP to be a proportionate means of achieving a legitimate aim (called the 'justification defence')

This is best illustrated with a (somewhat silly) example. Say Manfred owns a company and issues an advertisement inviting candidates to apply for the post of production manager. However, he stipulates that he will only recruit someone with a "deep, commanding voice" (thereby applying the PCP of voice pitch). That PCP would disproportionately disadvantage most women, as most women cannot be said to speak with a deep voice, an attribute usually associated with men. As Mildred is a woman (thereby sharing the protected characteristic of sex) and speaks with a higher-pitched voice, she would suffer the same disadvantage as most of the other women.

Manfred's reason is that he speaks with a deep voice and likes his senior managers to do the same as it creates a "masterful, commanding impression for staff and clients". That's probably not a legitimate aim, so Mildred is indirectly discriminated against in relation to her sex. Even if the aim was legitimate, Manfred's PCP would not be a proportionate means of achieving it.

Artificial intelligence

In a recruitment scenario, indirect discrimination is a real risk that may inadvertently fall under the radar. Each requirement for a role should therefore be analysed to ensure it is justifiable. The risk of indirect discrimination is particularly prevalent in the use of artificial intelligence (AI) tools, as they all use off-the-shelf algorithms with their own 'rules' that can amount to a PCP.

An algorithm is the set of rules that an AI process uses to carry out a task. At a very simple level, it may sort applications into order of date received, for example. However, in order for a more sophisticated tool to work, the algorithm needs to be fed a large corpus of data, so it can 'learn'. For example, it could be used to sift through hundreds of applications received in response to a job advertisement, looking for those that most closely fit the criteria for the role. The obvious risk with this, though, is that the output of the algorithm will be entirely dependent on the rules of the algorithm and the inputted data.

So, if the data is out of date from the point of view of what is acceptable recruitment practice, the results will be skewed or biased. For example, if a company enters data from the CVs of all of its successful hires between 2000 and 2020, it may well be the case that the algorithm will associate success with being male and white, and/or having attended an Oxbridge college. Obviously, a large business may have the resources to correct such biases, but a smaller business may not. In addition, many of these packages are developed in the United States where a different set of recruitment laws and conventions apply.

The obvious solution is to understand thoroughly how the AI tool works. If you do not, then an up-to-date British tool that expressly warrants that it complies with employment law and good practice is obviously to be preferred. Secondly, if possible, a cross-check should be carried out by a human, even if only done on a sample, to ensure the algorithm is working in line with the policies of the business, and with current laws and good practice.

Justification

As you saw above, indirect discrimination may be justified if the PCP is a proportionate means of achieving a legitimate end. Promoting health and safety particularly lends itself to satisfying the legitimate aim limb of the justification test, but others have included the upholding of political, philosophical or religious neutrality in a public-facing role and maintaining a high-quality personal service for customers. Cost-saving considerations can amount to a legitimate aim provided that it is not the only one (known as the 'cost plus' approach).

Be aware that it is not possible to justify direct discrimination, except in the case of age discrimination, where justification is available as a defence if the aim of the discriminatory measure relates to employment policy, the labour market or vocational training, and not purely individual reasons particular to the employee's situation.

There is a particular type of disability discrimination, apart from direct and indirect, which is where you **treat a disabled person unfavourably because of something arising in consequence of their disability**, where you cannot show that the treatment is a proportionate means of achieving a legitimate aim. In other words, this type of discrimination (called section 15 disability discrimination) can be justified.

Disability discrimination and reasonable adjustments

As well as being protected against direct and indirect discrimination, and from section 15 discrimination, you, as an employer or prospective employer, must make reasonable adjustments where:

- provisions, criteria or practices put a disabled person at a substantial disadvantage in relation to a relevant matter in comparison to people who are not disabled

- their premises have a physical feature that puts a disabled person at a substantial disadvantage

- their disabled employee will be put at a substantial disadvantage if they are not provided with an auxiliary aid

In a recruitment scenario, the duty to make reasonable adjustments extends to:

- the formats and media in which advertisements are published (so, for example, they are machine-readable for visually impaired people, if requested)

- the language used in written communications, such as job advertisements, job descriptions and person specifications application forms and tests (where fluency in English or high cognitive functioning is not required, the use of simpler English for people with learning difficulties should be used, for example)

- the accessibility of premises for interviews

- the environment and format in which the interview is to be held (so that people who are, say, neuro-divergent are not disadvantaged)

Of course, there are a near-infinite number of reasonable adjustments that could be made dependent on the nature of the disability and the circumstances, so you are not required to try to anticipate every possible situation in advance. However, job advertisements and application forms should carry a clear statement that reasonable adjustments will be made where the candidate indicates that it would be helpful or necessary.

Victimisation is defined in section 27 of the Equality Act 2010. It occurs when a person (A) subjects another person (B) to a detriment because B has done a 'protected act' or A believes that B has done or may do a protected act. A protected act is defined in the Equality Act 2010 as:

- bringing proceedings under the Equality Act 2010

- giving evidence or information in connection with proceedings under the Equality Act 2010

- doing any other thing for the purposes of or in connection with the Equality Act 2010

- making an allegation (whether or not express) that A or another person has contravened the Equality Act 2010

Harassment is defined in section 26 of the Equality Act 2010. It can be summarised as follows (conflating subsections (1) and (2)):

> *"A person (A) harasses another (B) if A engages in unwanted conduct related to a relevant protected characteristic, or of unwanted conduct of a sexual nature, and the conduct has the purpose or effect of violating B's dignity, or creating an intimidating, hostile, degrading, humiliating or offensive environment for B."*

There is an additional definition in subsection (3) relating to less favourable treatment where B rejects or submits to unwanted conduct of a sexual nature or that is related to gender reassignment or sex, and A treats B less favourably than A would treat B if B had not rejected or submitted to the conduct.

So, if an employer recruiting for a beauty consultant in a salon were to humiliate someone in a job interview because they had a facial disfigurement, for example (a facial disfigurement being capable of amounting to a disability under the Equality Act 2010), that could amount to unlawful harassment. A further example would be where an employer refused to employ a woman (or man) because they had refused a sexual advance during the interview.

Recruitment-specific sections of the Equality Act 2010

Sections 39 and 40 of the Equality Act 2010 address discrimination, victimisation and harassment against job applicants. Section 39(1) states that:

> *"An employer (A) must not discriminate against a person (B):*
>
> - *in the arrangements A makes for deciding to whom to offer employment*
>
> - *as to the terms on which A offers B employment and*
>
> - *by not offering B employment."*

Section 39(1) has a wide application because of the concept of 'arrangements', which has a broad interpretation. It covers all stages of the recruitment process, including the advertisement and job specification, the shortlisting process, the interview process and the decision-making stage. In particular, think about barriers that prevent people with certain characteristics from applying or make it harder for them. This could include:

- how the advertisement is worded, including requirements that exclude certain people

- where the advertisement is placed

- the place where or the time when the interview is scheduled to take place

- the manner in which the interview is conducted

I examine these issues further in the upcoming chapters.

Section 39(3) provides that the employer (A) must also not victimise a person (B):

- in the arrangements A makes for deciding to whom to offer employment

- as to the terms on which A offers B employment

- by not offering B employment

Section 40 states that an employer (A) must not, in relation to employment by A, harass a person who has applied to A for employment.

Who is responsible for discrimination in recruitment?

Liability can lie with you, the employer; an employee of the company; and/or a recruitment agent. Even if you do not instruct an employee or a recruitment agent to act in a discriminatory way, or do not endorse or condone the conduct, you can still be liable for the discriminatory acts unless you can show you took 'all reasonable steps' to prevent the action. If you can establish that defence, the employee or recruitment agent may still be personally liable.

To be able to establish this defence, you should provide training and express guidance to staff about how to conduct a recruitment exercise without discrimination, and you should provide an express instruction to your agents not to unlawfully discriminate. Training would include, as a minimum, guidance on your equality policy and how it applies to a recruitment situation. It may also include:

- how to draft the advertisements and job descriptions

- how to select candidates for interview

- how to carry out interviews

- how to assess candidates

- how any AI used in the recruitment process actually works, and its limitations and inherent risks

Throughout the recruitment process, you will need to bear in mind the dangers of unconscious bias and stereotyped assumptions.

You should obviously create and retain a paper trail to show the training and instructions you have given to employees, but you should also keep copies of everything created and received during the process. This will include:

- the advertisements

- the job descriptions and job specifications

- the notes made by staff who sift and select candidates for interview

- all interview notes, including questions asked and answers given, and panel discussions

- any tests and test results

- correspondence with candidates and between staff involved in the exercise

Obviously, the reason for keeping these documents is to be able to show that you have followed a discrimination-free process, and so you should be in a position to show them to third parties, including the candidate and their lawyer and the ET if necessary. Staff engaged in shortlisting and interviews should therefore avoid recording any comments that could suggest a discriminatory approach.

Under the UK General Data Protection Regulation (GDPR) and the Data Protection Act 2018, personal data about living individuals should be kept no longer than is necessary. How long that is depends on whether you receive a challenge to any aspect of the process. If not, a rule of thumb would be to keep everything for at least six months. Otherwise, in the case of an allegation of unlawful practice, you are justified in keeping data until the matter is resolved. Obviously, you would keep personal data about the person you have recruited for longer although, even then, there will be a point when that information is no longer necessary.

Summary

Discrimination law is a complex area, and I can only cover the main aspects in this book. A comprehensive publicly accessible resource is the excellent Statutory Code of Practice issued by the EHRC in January 2011 and supplemented in March and May 2014. The EHRC's website at www.equalityhumanrights.com also has a wealth of up-to-date resources, including guidance entitled "*What Equality Law Means for You as an Employer: When You Recruit Someone to Work For You*".

It is crucial to keep potential discrimination at the front of your mind at every step of the recruitment process, whether you are a large, well-resourced employer or a really small one. While few employers intentionally discriminate, many pitfalls can arise when you make choices about people. Always pause and think about whether your action could:

- exclude someone or a group of people

- unfairly favour someone or a group of people

- make it harder for someone compared to others

- make someone feel marginalised or unwanted

Of course, not every action resulting in these effects will amount to unlawful discrimination, but even if they do not, it is worth thinking about whether a certain approach could be counter-productive by artificially narrowing down your potential talent pool. I explore this a little more in Chapter 5.

Chapter 4
Data protection

An external recruitment exercise harvests a significant amount of personal information about people. The data is contained in CVs, completed application forms, equal opportunities monitoring responses, proficiency and psychometric test results, emails, texts and messages, social media searches, interview notes, offers of employment and draft employment contracts.

Some of the information is sensitive (known as special category data) and the recruiting business is a data controller for the purposes of the legislation. Therefore, it is crucial to understand the consequences of receiving all that data.

There are two pieces of legislation in the UK that currently deal with data protection. The retained EU law version of the GDPR and the Data Protection Act 2018. Note that the government is currently reviewing the UK's data protection laws with a view to making them more business-friendly, although at the time of writing (June 2022) they have not yet published the results of the public consultation process that closed in November 2021.

It's important to start by defining some key terms:

Personal data is any information relating to an identified or identifiable living individual. This encompasses a potentially vast range of information in a recruitment context, such as names, schools attended, qualifications, work history, affiliations, contact details, health conditions and other personal characteristics, to name but a few.

A data subject is an identifiable living person to whom the personal data relates. Anyone supplying information about themselves, either speculatively or in response to a job advertisement, will be a data subject, and they will be subject to the protections of the UK's data protection laws.

A data controller is a natural or legal person, public authority, agency or other body that alone or jointly determines the purposes and means of the processing of personal data. This will include any organisation that receives personal data during a recruitment process.

Processing means carrying out an operation or set of operations on personal data, either manually or automatically. This definition has a very wide scope and includes (by way of example only):

- collecting, recording, organising or storing data

- retrieving and using data

- adapting, amending or combining data

- transmitting, disseminating or otherwise disclosing data

- restricting, destroying or amending data

Special category personal data relates to sensitive information, of which processing is prohibited unless an exception applies. This category comprises information about:

- racial or ethnic origin

- political opinions

- religious or philosophical beliefs

- trade union membership

- genetic data

- biometric data for the purpose of unique identification

- health data

- data about a person's sex life or sexual orientation

While most businesses would not deliberately choose to collect and otherwise process these types of special category information during a recruitment exercise, it is possible to end up with such information accidentally.

Special circumstances apply in relation to processing personal data relating to criminal convictions and offences. I examine these in Chapter 12.

Because of the very wide definition of processing and of personal data, an organisation carrying out a recruitment exercise will fall within the scope of the data protection laws. This means that they will have to comply with the seven **data protection principles**. In summary, these principles are that personal data:

- has to be processed **lawfully, fairly and in a transparent way**

- must only be collected for **specified, explicit and legitimate purposes** and not processed any further in a way that is incompatible with those purposes

- must be **adequate, relevant and limited to what is necessary** in relation to the purposes for which it is processed

- must be **accurate** and, where necessary, **kept up to date**. Inaccurate data must be **rectified or erased**

- must be **kept for no longer than is necessary** for the purposes for which it is processed

- must be processed in a way that **ensures appropriate security**, including protection against unauthorised or unlawful processing and accidental loss, destruction or damage

The principle of **accountability** requires that the data controller is responsible for and must be able to show compliance with the other principles.

What allows an organisation to process data in a recruitment scenario? The UK GDPR allows processing in six situations only, called the Article 6 conditions. The four that are likely to be relevant to recruitment are where:

- the data subject has **given consent** to the processing of their personal data for one or more specific purposes.

- the processing is **necessary for the performance of a contract** to which the data subject is a party or in order to take steps at the request of a data subject prior to entering into a contract.

- the processing is **necessary to comply with a legal obligation** to which the controller is subject.

- the processing is **necessary for the purposes of the controller's legitimate interests** or those pursued by a third party, except where those interests are overridden by the interest and fundamental rights and freedoms of the data subject, which require protection of personal data.

Consent is not considered a safe condition to rely on in an employment scenario because employment relationships are not based on equality of power, and so the consent to the processing of data may not be seen as a freely given, specific, informed and unambiguous indication of the data subject's wishes.

It is not safe to argue that the consent is implied when the candidate has sent in their personal data in response to an advertisement, as the candidate will not know exactly how their personal data will be stored, who will see it or how it will be used. It is always better to try to rely on one of the other reasons, below.

The performance of a contract condition is one relied on significantly by employers in relation to their existing staff, and the pre-contractual limb of the condition may be relevant in a recruitment scenario when an offer has been made and negotiations are ongoing between you and the preferred candidate. However, guidance from the Information Commissioner's Office (ICO) indicates that this condition cannot be relied on where the pre-contractual steps have been taken on your initiative or that of a third party. Therefore, this will only help where the candidate has supplied the personal data being processed as part of the pre-contractual steps being taken.

Compliance with a legal obligation will include the statutory, regulatory and common law obligations that you are subject to. In a recruitment situation, it could include pre-employment vetting to ensure that the candidate has the right to work in the UK or vetting of candidates who would be subject to the senior manager and certification regime applying to employers authorised under the Financial Services and Markets Act 2000.

The legitimate interests category is arguably the most flexible for organisations engaged in recruitment. Because of the limitation inherent in this category, in relation to the interests and fundamental rights and freedoms of the data subject, processing carried out for this reason must be done proportionately and in the least intrusive way possible.

Guidance from the ICO identifies that, in order to use this reason, the controller must:

- identify a legitimate interest, which could be its own or another person's, including the data subject's

- show that the processing in question is necessary to achieve the legitimate interest

- balance it against the individual's interests and fundamental rights and freedoms

An obvious example in a recruitment context is collecting information about a candidate's qualifications and experience. The processing could typically include storing the information, extracting parts of it, copying the information for the interview panel and then later deleting it. The legitimate purpose for processing this information is to enable you to assess the candidate's suitability for employment and for the role in question. The processing as described is necessary to achieve that legitimate interest, and it is not likely to infringe the candidate's fundamental rights and freedoms.

However, let's say an over-enthusiastic manager shares the candidate's CV with his entire department of 40 people, asking for feedback and comments. That is likely to fall outside the scope of what could be regarded as necessary to achieve the legitimate interest of assessing suitability. The action would likely be seen as excessive and disproportionate.

Special category personal data needs careful consideration. When you hold special category personal data about an individual, you must ensure that the appropriate conditions are met (set out in Part 1 of Schedule 1 of the Data Protection Act 2018. The conditions are:

- the processing is **necessary for the purposes of performing or exercising obligations or rights** which are imposed or conferred by law on the employer or employee in connection with employment.

- when the processing is carried out, **the employer has an appropriate policy** in place.

- the employer must **keep a record of processing activities**, including:

- that the condition relied on is that processing is necessary for the purposes of performing or exercising obligations or rights of the employer or data subject which are imposed or conferred by law

- whether the personal data is retained and erased in accordance with the employer's policies and, if not, the reason

- how one or more of the Article 6 conditions are met.

These safeguards, along with those relating to the policy document, are known as the **Part 4 additional safeguards**.

The **policy document** referred to must explain your procedures for complying with the data protection principles in connection with the processing of the data and your policies regarding the retention and erasing of personal data, indicating how long the data is likely to be kept.

For the period beginning when you start to carry out processing and ending six months after you cease such processing, you must:

- retain the appropriate policy document

- review it and, where appropriate, update it from time to time

- make it available to the ICO without charge upon request

These are also part of the **Part 4 additional safeguards**.

For example, you can legitimately process special category personal data in a recruitment context where a role has certain minimal health needs, such as certain eyesight or hearing requirements.

Another condition enabling the processing of special category personal information relates to **race equality**.

You can also process special category personal data (including data about an individual's criminal convictions and offences committed) where the employee or candidate has **given their express consent**, or where one of the **substantial public interest conditions** set out in Part 2 of Schedule 1 of the Data Protection Act 2018 have been met (provided that an appropriate policy document is in place, along with the additional safeguards set out in Part 4 of Schedule 1).

The **substantial public interest conditions** are:

- administration of justice

- preventing fraud

- terrorism or money laundering

- equality of opportunity or treatment

- specific circumstances

In my view, most of the substantial public interest conditions are unlikely to apply in most recruitment situations. One that could apply relates to equality of opportunity or treatment, where the data reveals racial or ethnic origins, religious or philosophical beliefs or concerns about health or sexual orientation. The processing must be for the purpose of identifying or keeping under review the existence or absence of **equality of opportunity or treatment** between specified groups, with a view to enabling such equality to be promoted or maintained. In addition, this exception does not apply where:

- the processing is carried out for the purposes of measures or decisions regarding a specific data subject

- the processing is likely to cause substantial distress or damage to an individual

- the data subject has served written notice to stop processing their personal data

Another specific public interest condition is set out in paragraph 9 of Part 2 of Schedule 1 of the Data Protection Act 2018, where the processing is carried out as part of a process of identifying suitable individuals to hold senior positions in an organisation. A senior position is a director, secretary or similar officer; a member of an LLP; a partner; or a senior manager who has a significant role in making decisions about how an organisation's activities are to be managed or organised.

Privacy notices

In their capacity as data controllers, recruiters and employers have an obligation under the UK GDPR to provide information to candidates and staff (whether employees, contractors or agency workers) about any personal data about them that is to be collected and processed. There is no prescribed way of doing this, but the most convenient way is probably to issue a Privacy Notice (also known as a Fair Processing Notice).

The Privacy Notice has to cover the following information:

- the organisation's name and contact details
- the names and contact details of the organisation's representative and data protection officer
- the purposes of the processing
- the lawful basis for the processing
- what legitimate interests you are relying on
- the categories of personal data
- where the personal data will be obtained from

- who will receive the personal data

- details of any transfers of the personal data overseas

- how long the personal data will be kept

- the rights of the individual in relation to the processing

- the right of the individual to withdraw consent to the processing, if consent has been given

- the right to complain to the ICO

- the details of whether individuals are under a statutory or contractual obligation to provide the personal data (if it is collected from the individual it relates to)

- the details of any automated decision-making, including profiling, if relevant

This information has to be given to the individual when you collect personal data from them, or within a month of obtaining it if you get it from another source. If you plan to disclose the personal data to a third party, the data subject must be advised of that no later than when the information is disclosed.

There are some exceptions to when you have to provide privacy information, including where the individual already has it, where it would be impossible to provide it or where it would involve a disproportionate effort.

You can also withhold the information if doing so would render the achievement of the objectives of the processing impossible or seriously impair it. For example, this might be the case if you are recording the movements of staff in order to try to detect who is responsible for a spate of thefts.

The privacy information you provide must be concise, transparent, intelligible, easily accessible and use clear and plain language. In other words, you must not use technical jargon or be misleading, and you must ensure that the information is easy to locate.

Because the Privacy Notice has to be 'meaningful', it must be tailored for the type of business, the kinds of personal data being processed, how it is processed, and the individuals it will be given to. For example, the notice you give to employees is likely to be quite different from the notice you give to casual independent contractors, for whom far fewer types of information are likely to be held.

Chapter 5
The advertisement and job description

Advertisements

The job advertisement is a key document, as it is the bait that will hook the right candidate. Before placing an external advertisement, consider whether you should try to find the new post holder internally first. This is necessary where the business is engaged in a redundancy situation, and there are employees who could avoid dismissal by being redeployed. Where an employee has been selected for redundancy while they are on maternity leave or shared parental leave, they have a right to be offered any suitable vacancies.

Redundancy situations aside, to avoid discrimination claims, people away from work on parental leave or long-term sick leave should be advised of any vacancies.

While only advertising internally will save money and time, remember that it may also risk entrenching a lack of diversity in the workforce. Recruiting externally will obviously make a far greater pool of potential candidates available.

While being the 'bait' to attract good candidates, the job advertisement should also be accurate, if only because a misleading advertisement will result in unsuitable applicants or disappointed and disaffected candidates. In particular, any significant terms and conditions governing the role should be mentioned, including whether the role is permanent or fixed-term; full- or part-time; based at home, in the office or in a hybrid arrangement; or whether it requires extensive travelling.

From the perspective of where you will place the advertisement, industry-specific publications and websites may be an obvious first step, but they may not be the best place if you are looking for entry-level or non-specialist staff. There is a vast range of different avenues for seeking staff nowadays, and a carefully targeted approach is often needed to ensure you are not wasting time and money.

However, a targeted approach may inadvertently end up excluding potentially valuable candidates and restricting your talent pool, as well as amounting to indirect discrimination. It may feel intuitive or even safe to seek to recruit 'people like us', or people who clearly fit the corporate culture, but there is significant research showing that truly diverse workforces are more entrepreneurial, innovative and talented than more traditionally constituted ones.

Think about who is most likely to read or be attracted to the medium you have chosen. Advertisements posted solely on social media are likely to exclude older people and those without access to the internet. Some publications may mainly reach certain genders, age groups, ethnic groups or sexual orientations, even if that is not your intention.

I examined positive action in the last chapter and explained when an organisation is allowed to practise it. The EHRC gives examples of positive action that organisations can take to address the effects of pre-existing discrimination. The recruitment-specific examples are:

- placing job advertisements targeting particular groups to increase the number of applicants from those groups

- including statements in job advertisements to encourage applications from under-represented groups, such as, "We welcome female applicants"

- favouring the job candidate from an under-represented group, where two candidates are 'as qualified as' each other

For some years, it was thought that an individual could not bring a claim against an employer in relation to a discriminatory job advertisement as it would merely indicate an intention to discriminate rather than an act of discrimination. However, two decisions of the European Court of Justice (the ECJ) suggest that this approach cannot be sustained. The 2008 case of *Centrum voor Gelijkheid van Kansen en voor Racismebestrijding v NV Firma Feryn* involved a Belgian employer that stated publicly that they would not employ people from Morocco. The ECJ found that this was direct discrimination in contravention of the Race Directive because it deterred Moroccans from applying for a post they knew they would not be appointed to.

A case decided ten years later (*AH v Associazione Avvocatura per I diritti LGBTI*) involved statements made by a lawyer on an Italian radio station that he would never hire a gay person. The ECJ said that, although there was no active recruitment happening at the time, the statement could still hinder access to employment, and so was capable of falling within the scope of the Equal Treatment Framework Directive 2000/78, although the link between the public statements of this kind and the conditions for access to employment must not be hypothetical.

Since the 2008 case, there have been two contradictory Employment Appeal Tribunal (EAT) decisions. In *Berry v Recruitment Revolution and others*, decided in 2010, the EAT accepted that a discriminatory advertisement could amount to 'arrangements for recruitment' under the former equivalent of section 39 of the Equality Act 2010, although the EAT did not have to decide the matter. In the other, *Ruhanza v Alexander Hancock Recruitment Ltd*, decided in 2012, the EAT ruled that a claim in relation to a discriminatory advertisement could only be brought by the Equality and Human Rights Commission (EHRC) and not by an individual.

The EHRC is empowered to investigate whether a person has committed an unlawful act, and the body can also apply for an injunction where it believes that someone is likely to commit an unlawful act under the Equality Act 2006. This would include the publishing of an advertisement demonstrating an intention to discriminate. Section 24A(3) of the Equality Act 2006 states that an unlawful act "includes making arrangements to act in a particular way which would, if applied to an individual, amount to unlawful discrimination". No actual victim need be identified.

It is not likely that placing an advertisement in a medium targeted at a certain type of person would fall foul of the Equality Act 2010 on its own. Just because only a certain age group tends to read a specific publication, say, will not found a claim provided that other age groups have the same unrestricted access to it. However, an organisation that tended to place job advertisements in such a publication may find their practice being cited as evidence to support an age discrimination claim against them.

Successful claims are much more likely to be made based on the contents of job advertisements. An advertisement that expressly or impliedly seeks to exclude someone falling within one of the nine protected characteristics will be evidence of unlawful direct discrimination, unless the job falls within a genuine occupational requirement or qualification – see below for more about this.

For example, an advertisement seeking "a fit young man" or "a mature and able-bodied Christian" would be clear evidence of a multi-dimensional directly discriminatory practice (unless one of the exceptions applies). Using words such as 'salesman' or 'waitress' will be discriminatory, as will wording such as 'would suit a new graduate', 'recent retiree sought' and 'sales staff with flawless complexions required'.

Genuine occupational requirements

Apart from taking positive action to redress the effects of inherent discrimination, you can expressly seek candidates with certain protected characteristics where that is a genuine requirement of the job. This is allowed when the requirement is an occupational requirement and the application of the requirement is a proportionate means of achieving a legitimate aim.

You are therefore allowed to reject someone in these circumstances when the person does not meet the requirement (or you have reasonable grounds for not being satisfied that the person meets the requirement). An example would be where a care worker is required to bathe and toilet women. In that case, you can specifically advertise for a female care worker.

There is an express exception set out in Schedule 9 of the Equality Act 2010 allowing you to impose a requirement for a person to be of a particular sex or not to be a transsexual person, or relating to marriage, civil partnership or sexual orientation requirements where the employment is for the purposes of an organised religion, provided other conditions are satisfied. This is a niche area that goes beyond the scope of this book.

However, the Equality Act 2010 also addresses the situation where you have an ethos based on religion or belief. In order to be able to take advantage of the genuine occupational requirement exception, you would have to be able to demonstrate that, having regard to that ethos and the nature or context of the work, having a particular religion or belief is an occupational requirement, and the application of the requirement is a proportionate means of achieving a legitimate aim.

An example would be a kindergarten that was founded and operates in accordance with the principles of Islam, and which could require that an assistant was a practising Muslim. Note that this exception in section 3 of Schedule 9 does not allow a religious or belief-based organisation to discriminate against people with other characteristics, such as sexual orientation or marriage.

If you are seeking to reply on a genuine occupational requirement to reject someone who would otherwise be able to carry out the role, you should examine carefully whether some of the duties could be carried out by the person, with the restricted duties being done by an existing staff member who has the required characteristic. You should carefully note your justification for rejecting the person.

Job descriptions and person specifications

Of course, if you are recruiting to replace someone, you will probably have the job description and person specification already to hand. It is still worth checking them to ensure they accurately reflect the needs of the business and the day-to-day reality of the role. In addition, you may anticipate that the role will change over time, in which case you will want to ensure that the job description is drafted flexibly, to accommodate those anticipated changes.

However, you should avoid including descriptions of the role that are unnecessary and could put off potential candidates, especially if such descriptions could create a provision, criterion or practice that disadvantages a person or group. For example, if the role only requires overtime to be worked very occasionally, I recommend not stating that overtime working is required, as it could discourage working mothers from applying, creating a risk of indirect discrimination. Similarly, describing a role as full-time when it could be worked as a job share would potentially deter working mothers.

Person specification

While the job description describes the role, the job specification describes the qualifications and attributes of the ideal candidate. This document therefore has the potential to exclude candidates by focusing on qualities that some categories of people cannot fulfil. Here are some examples:

- "A youthful mindset is required". This could put off older people. It would be better to state: "A flexible mindset is required".

- "A high level of physical fitness is needed for this active and physical role" This would exclude most people with physical disabilities, many of whom might be able to do the job in practice with reasonable adjustments. It would be better to omit the reference to "physical fitness" and to describe the tasks accurately in the job description so that potential candidates can judge their suitability themselves.

- "We are looking for someone with at least five years' continuous experience in sales". This could discourage women who have taken a career break to have children and younger people. It is better to exclude the reference to specific years of experience and to describe instead what the person would have to be able to do. It would be ok just to say "An experienced salesperson".

- "Five GCSEs at C grade or above are required". This could exclude people who were educated overseas or older people who did not take GSCEs. It is better to add "or equivalent qualifications".

Chapter 6
Sifting the applications and shortlisting

Application forms

Provided that they do not ask discriminatory questions or disadvantage categories of people (such as visually impaired people) in other ways, the use of an application form has the advantage of standardising the recruitment process so that every candidate provides the same categories of information, making the assessment and decision process much easier to process and justify.

The public sector and some private businesses now use 'blind' assessments to help avoid unconscious or deliberate biases. For example, details such as age, gender, name and schools attended can be omitted, making it harder for assessors to be unconsciously influenced by irrelevant factors.

When sifting applications and CVs, you need to decide in advance what criteria to use and how to weight them. For example, if experience in the industry is crucial, then that should be weighted most heavily.

A scoring system will help to ensure consistency in assessments. Adversely weighting criteria that could be discriminatory should be avoided if possible. These include:

- gaps in employment history (where a person may have been engaged in child care or ill)

- unfamiliar qualifications (such as those gained overseas, or many years ago)

- being 'over-qualified', which could amount to age discrimination

Obviously, criteria based on protected characteristics, such as age, sex and sexual orientation, must be avoided unless you can rely on a genuine occupational requirement argument, or you can identify a justifiable proportionate aim in the case of age.

Some organisations use tests or other assessment tools, such as psychometric or proficiency testing. The same cautionary approach is necessary to ensure that people are not directly or indirectly discriminated against because of their protected characteristics. For example, instructions should be easy to understand for people who do not speak fluent English.

Where someone has identified that they need reasonable adjustments in the recruitment process, that will extend to the tests. Adjustments may include:

- having tests in braille, large font or machine-readable format

- enabling candidates to use a reader or scribe

- being flexible in the way the test is presented and taken

- ensuring the test centre is accessible

The safest approach is to ask candidates what adjustments they may need. Clearly, an adjustment that would give the disabled person an unfair advantage, such as enabling them to collaborate with someone in working out the answers, can be refused, but where that is not a likely outcome of an adjustment, I recommend giving the candidate the benefit of the doubt.

Chapter 7

Interview(s) and the decision-making process

Having shortlisted the candidates for interview, you will need to:

- decide who will conduct the interviews. This could be an internal manager and/or HR or an external interviewer. Beware of perceived or actual bias if one of the candidates is managed by, or a friend or relative of the interviewer

- decide how many stages will be required for the interview process

- decide how the interviews will be conducted. They could be wholly online or at a physical location, such as at the organisation's offices, or a combination of the two

- decide what the selection criteria will be, and what questions are to be asked

- contact the shortlisted candidates to advise them of their interview; the process; and the time, date and location

When contacting the candidates, advise them of the format of the interviews, who will be conducting them and the possible timescale. You should always enquire as to whether they need any special arrangements or reasonable adjustments to be made. For example, some candidates may need to use a sign language interpreter or bring certain equipment. Not all adjustments will relate to a disability. For example, some candidates may need to leave in time to pick up their children or be home by sunset on a Friday for religious reasons.

Just as using template selection criteria can help to ensure consistency in sifting and shortlisting, this approach can also be valuable when conducting interviews. For example, a template could be divided into the following parts:

- a short introduction by the lead interviewer so that the same information is given to each candidate

- a set of questions to be asked of each interviewee that is designed to ascertain their suitability

- a tailored set of questions that relate to the specifics of each candidate's CV or application form. These should be kept to a minimum and used to address concerns or seek clarifications

- an invitation to ask questions of the panel

- a summary of the process from that point on

While consistency is valuable, it should not be followed slavishly. A given set of questions may work for most candidates, but be mindful of those who do not fit the usual mould. For example, a candidate who is much older or younger than most of the other interviewees, or one who grew up abroad may need to be asked slightly different questions.

The decision

Many experienced interviewers will 'go with their gut' when deciding who to select. This has much to recommend it where the interviewer has a very good feel for the role being filled and the sort of skill set that is needed. However, it is important not to fall foul of stereotyped assumptions and unconscious biases when adopting this approach. The interviewers may envisage an ideal post holder, but that ideal may correspond with certain characteristics that are actually irrelevant to the person's ability to do the job.

Unconscious bias can be very subtle and especially hard to detect in oneself. It may relate to any number of characteristics, such as accent, timbre of voice, social background, age, gender, race or appearance – in fact, anything that you may consider to be part of 'fitting in'. Everyone has an unconscious bias about something – it's all part of being a human being – and one person's pet hate could be another's delight. Does the candidate pronounce 'H' as 'aitch' or 'haitch'? (Everyone believes those using the other pronunciation are wrong.) Maybe the candidate reminds you of your father – that could be a positive or a negative thing.

The important thing is to think carefully about why you prefer one candidate over another. Identify the characteristics you are judging (positively or negatively) and really think critically about why they are relevant. If you think they are not, ignore them and appraise the candidates again. Having objectively verifiable selection criteria in the first place will greatly assist in this.

The rejection

Always be considerate of candidates and let them know if they are not successful in good time. In a job market with a short supply of good candidates, and with social media enabling the rapid dissemination of all sorts of opinions and information, organisations cannot afford to get a reputation for treating candidates (and by extension, staff) shoddily.

Your rejection letters and emails should be courteous and friendly, no matter how disastrous you thought the interview was. If you are contacted for feedback, give it (in a constructive way) if you can do so without risking a discrimination claim. It's generally best to send carefully formulated feedback in writing rather than giving off-the-cuff views by telephone. Do not engage in an extended exchange with the rejected candidate though.

Chapter 8
The right to work in the United Kingdom

One aspect of the recruitment process that can cause headaches is ensuring that the preferred candidate has the legal right to work in the UK (without discriminating because of their race, ethnic origin or nationality). The rules are complex and change frequently, so this chapter can only give an overview of the position as it stood in June 2022. If in any doubt, you should seek professional advice from an immigration specialist.

There are at least 15 pieces of legislation relating to immigration currently in force, as well as the detailed Immigration Rules and Operational Guidance published by the Home Office. The Immigration Rules set out the provisions for the categories of people who can apply for leave to enter and work in the UK, as well as the grounds for refusing that leave and the rights of appeal. The guidance notes explain how the Immigration Rules are applied and interpreted. These notes are available on the government website of the UK Visa and Immigration division (UKVI).

Because of the complexities and 'red tape' involved in obtaining permission for a migrant to work in the UK, you should be prepared to wait several weeks, or even months, before the requisite permissions are granted. Many factors are involved, including the country the person submits their application in, the time of year and the specifics of the person's circumstances.

What you have to do

You must prevent illegal working or face severe criminal and civil penalties. These include a fine of up to £20,000 per worker illegally employed and a prison sentence of up to five years where you had reasonable cause to believe that the person was being employed illegally. It is therefore crucial that you take all reasonable steps to satisfy yourself that the preferred candidate has the right to work in the UK.

Broadly speaking, the following people have the right to work in the UK without specific permission:

- British citizens
- citizens of the Republic of Ireland
- EEA and Swiss nationals who have been granted settled status, and their non-EU family members who have a right of residence
- people with the right of abode

- people with indefinite leave to remain, permanent residence or settlement status

- people with refugee status

- certain asylum seekers, although the employment may be restricted

- certain overseas students (up to 20 hours per week during term time and full-time during holidays)

Most other categories of people need specific permission to work in the UK, including citizens of British Dependent Territories, British nationals and British overseas citizens.

People needing specific permission to work in the UK

The majority of migrants will obtain their permission by first being sponsored by their employer. To sponsor a migrant, you, as the employer (being an organisation or sole trader, rather than an individual), need to hold a sponsorship licence granted by the Home Office. A sponsor is then able to access an online Sponsor Management System and assign a Certificate of Sponsorship to a worker in respect of a specific role.

Before granting a licence, the Home Office will satisfy itself that you have appropriate HR and recruitment systems in place, have an appropriate workplace, and have appropriate contracts with any third parties at whose site the migrant worker may be located.

Before granting permission to work to a specific migrant worker, the Home Office will want to be satisfied that role is genuine, that the migrant has the requisite skills to undertake it and that the role will pay an appropriate rate. Other criteria will also need to be met by the migrant worker.

If you are granted a sponsor's licence, you take on a significant amount of responsibility, including acting in accordance with immigration and employment legislation and undertaking reporting and record-keeping activities. Failure to do this, or otherwise acting against the public good, can result in sanctions, including the suspension, downgrading or revocation of the licence.

The **record-keeping duties** of a sponsor include keeping copies of migrant workers' biometric permits and right to work in the UK, terms and conditions of employment and up- to-date contact information. The documentation in respect of any given migrant worker must be kept for a year from the date the sponsorship of the worker ended, unless a Home Office compliance officer has already approved the information since the sponsorship ended.

In a recruitment scenario, the types of workers who need to be sponsored are 'skilled workers' and temporary workers.

To qualify under the skilled worker route, the candidate must score enough points. This entails:

- the candidate meeting minimum English language and maintenance requirements

- the role being skilled to at least RQF level 3 (equivalent to A level)

- the role paying at least £25,600 a year (or the going rate for the role if higher). This criterion can be relaxed if the migrant is a new entrant to the labour market, the role is a shortage occupation or the candidate holds a relevant PhD

Employers have to pay an Immigration Fees Charge of £1,000 per skilled worker per year (unless you are a charity or small company). There are certain situations where the fee is waived, such as where the appointment is for less than six months or the migrant has a PhD. This fee must not be passed on to the migrant.

Sponsored temporary workers fall into a closed list of categories including:

- charity workers

- creative and sporting workers

- religious workers

People between the ages of 18 and 30 from a number of countries (such as Australia, New Zealand, Canada, Hong Kong and Japan) may work in the UK for up to two years provided they have been sponsored by their own countries.

Citizens of Commonwealth countries who have at least one grandparent born in the UK do not need sponsorship to work in the UK.

Graduates on a Tier 4 visa or Student visa who have completed a course of study in the UK can apply for a Graduate visa as long as they apply prior to the expiry of their existing visa. People with a PhD or other doctoral qualifications are granted a three-year visa and other graduates get a two-year visa. These time frames cannot be extended and the person must apply to switch to another type of visa to stay in the UK.

Dependants of work visa holders are generally entitled to work and can switch to the Skilled Worker category.

Important Note: After the proofs of this book were signed off, the first certified digital identity service provider for right to work checks was announced by the UK Government. This means more employers may now choose to roll out digital right to work checks for holders of valid UK and Irish passports (including Irish passport cards). Search online for 'digital online right to work checks' for more information.

Chapter 9
The offer of employment

The offer of employment sets out the terms of the proposed employment (often including a draft contract and other information) that the successful candidate is invited to consider and formally accept.

From a contractual point of view, the prospective employee may negotiate the terms offered and, if the negotiations are successful, any agreed changes should be carefully noted. Often, a revised contract will be issued. Until the candidate communicates their acceptance of the offer (or revised offer), you may withdraw it at any time.

Conditional offers of employment

If you wish to obtain satisfactory references or other information prior to confirming the appointment, you must make the offer conditional upon those contingencies being satisfied. Otherwise, if the potential employee accepts an unconditional offer, you cannot withdraw it later without breaching the contract. Whether that is serious or not will depend on the loss sustained by the candidate. Someone who resigns and moves to a different part of the country relying upon an unconditional offer, for example, could suffer tens of thousands of pounds of direct and indirect loss.

In order to safeguard against this risk, where you wish the candidate to start work before the information is obtained (where this is possible), you should stipulate in the contract that, under circumstances where unsatisfactory references are obtained (for example), the usual notice period will be curtailed and termination can occur immediately. You should make clear that 'unsatisfactory' means unsatisfactory to you, the employer, as it is a subjective matter. I examine how to deal with an unsatisfactory reference in Chapter 11 (although I touch on it in the next chapter also).

The types of information you may wish to check prior to confirming an offer include:

- references from former employers

- police and other checks

- health information

- the right to work in the UK

Chapter 10
Pre-employment screening

Guest chapter by Mike Clyne, FeMan Consulting
www.femanconsulting.co.uk

Why would you undertake employee screening?

Imagine the scenario: you are going on holiday and want someone to look after your house. You decide to put an advert online, you speak to a couple of people and pick someone. They show up as your bags are packed and you give them your keys, your Wi-Fi password, your bank account logins and copies of all your most important documents. Sounds far-fetched, doesn't it? If you hire an employee without doing any background checks, then you are leaving yourself open to an increased risk. The risk could be fraud risk, data risk, information security risk and/or reputational risk.

An organisation may undertake background checks because it is a regulated business (e.g., a financial firm regulated by the FCA), because investors require it, because the organisation's clients would expect it as part of their due diligence or, best of all, to manage its 'people risk'.

Background screening is not an MI5-level check. It is a series of additional data points that may indicate whether you have a prospective employee that may not be all they seem. All organisations face the risk of employee fraud, but the smaller the entity, the wider the span of access to information any individual will have. Therefore, these are the organisations that should be very keen to do proper checks.

What elements can you include in employee screening?

Any organisation wanting to carry out background checks should ensure that the checks are proportionate to the role and are applied consistently. Just deciding to do a screening because 'the candidate looks a bit dodgy' is likely to put you on the receiving end of a discrimination claim.

Elements that could be included:

- previous employment check (including dates of employment, job title, etc.)

- education check (did they *really* get a First from Oxford?)

- credit check (note: these are not creditworthiness checks but a check on whether an individual has an outstanding County Court Judgement or has been made bankrupt)

- criminal check (see later)

- global compliance watchlist check (to see if they are on a sanctions list or no-fly list, or if they are a politically exposed person)

- adverse media check (not just a Google search but a check on news databases to see if they are mentioned in connection with anything adverse)

- professional qualifications check

- directorships and disqualified directorships check (you'd want to know if someone had other interests that may lead to a conflict)

- ID check (to make sure the documents the individual presents to you, such as a passport, are not fake and are registered to them)

- driving licence check (if the prospective employee will be driving in their role)

- checks on adverse uses of social media (see below)

- CV check (compare the individual to the CV they gave during the application process)

What type of criminal checks are available?

Criminal record checks are covered in detail in Chapter 12. In summary, there are three levels of criminal check.

The Basic level check is available to anyone. It shows any unspent convictions and conditional cautions.

The Standard level check shows spent and unspent convictions and cautions. This is only available to specific roles (e.g., a senior manager in an FCA-regulated business, a solicitor or barrister, a vet, etc.).

The Enhanced level check is the same as a Standard level check, but it also includes any information that is relevant to the role (generally for roles that involve work with children or vulnerable adults).

Would undertaking an adverse use of social media check contravene an individual's right to privacy?

If you apply such checks consistently across all new employees and you can show the reason you are running them (i.e., to check for anything serious rather than just snooping), then you shouldn't have any issues. Many organisations undertake their own attempts at social media checks, which run the risk of inconsistencies. A proper outsourced provider will check against a number of areas (e.g., promotion or undertaking of illegal activity and evidence of hate speech, violence or extremist views, etc.) and then raise any concerns in a consistent way.

Organisations may be cautious about 'prying' into this aspect of an individual's life, but as stated earlier, you need to have a wide range of data points for your hiring decision. A prospective employee who is indiscreet about company information, talks about drug-taking or posts discriminatory material, for example, could cause you serious reputational risk.

You will also need to ensure that you are not discriminating against individuals by making judgements on their political beliefs or social activities, which are not relevant to the checks.

How do you allow for 'youthful indiscretions' so as not to blight someone's whole career?

Maybe this should be titled 'The Right to Have Been Stupid'. When an organisation reviews any flags raised on the checks, they should allow individuals who posted bad language 10 years earlier, during a night out with friends, to cleanse their social media history. Organisations should balance the time elapsed and the nature of the inappropriate material when making a judgement.

Should applicants be told in advance that they will be required to undertake background screening?

Yes. The organisation should be very open and explain why the screening will be done, setting out the elements of the screening that will be conducted.

Are employment references worth anything? Aren't they just anodyne?

Nowadays, you are more likely to get a 'dates only' reference, and less likely to get a fulsome reference that details the strengths and weaknesses of the individual. However the dates of employment and job title are important data points – do they match what the individual declared on their CV?

References are covered in detail in Chapter 11.

Is screening just for new employees?

No. You may decide that it is prudent to undertake ongoing screenings for individuals already hired. Clearly, you won't need to redo references for previous employment or education again, but you may wish to recheck credit and criminal checks among other elements.

Chapter 11
Seeking references

Many employers make offers of employment contingent upon receipt of satisfactory references, otherwise known as conditional offers. There are a number of reasons for obtaining references from a prospective employee, including:

- to comply with a statutory requirement (applicable in specified regulated sectors where an assessment of fitness and propriety is required)

- to satisfy yourself that their representations in their CV or application form are accurate

- to ascertain whether they were reliable and honest in their last role

- to find out why they left their last employment

- to find out dates of parental leave taken (due to the aggregating of the parental leave entitlement across employers)

You should independently check the contact and job role details of referees, as it is sadly not unknown for candidates to give the names of friends or relatives who pretend to be their former manager or employer. Do not just rely on written references either, as these can easily be faked.

Be clear whether the reference you have received is a reference made on behalf of the employer (sometimes called a corporate reference) or a personal reference from a former manager. References on headed notepaper and/or provided by HR are likely to be made on behalf of the employer.

Many employers now do not give references, other than to confirm dates of employment and position held or similar barebones factual information. There is no obligation on most employers to provide a reference, which is one of the reasons that some prospective employers carry out their own research on social media and the like.

Unsatisfactory references

I recommend a cautious approach before deciding to withdraw an offer or dismiss (where the employee has already started) and to ensure that the information you rely on does not amount to unlawful discrimination. For example, if the previous employer tells you that the employee had a lot of time off sick, make careful enquiries of the employee before deciding that withdrawal or dismissal is appropriate, as your withdrawal or dismissal could amount to direct discrimination on grounds of disability, or section 15 discrimination, as well as a failure to make reasonable adjustments.

In addition, the former employer may be malicious or have unlawful motives for giving an unfavourable reference. While taking a bad reference from a former employer at face value may not get you into legal trouble, it may cause you to miss out on employing a good employee who just happened not to get on with their former manager. This is another reason for drilling down with the prospective employee as to why a bad reference has been given.

Under the UK GDPR and the Data Protection Act 2018, a data subject can request access to personal information held about them, which will include information given in references. However, under paragraph 24 of schedule 2 of the Data Protection Act 2018, personal data can be withheld where it consists of a reference given or to be given in confidence for the purposes of:

- the education, training or employment (or prospective education, training or employment) of the data subject

- the placement (or prospective placement) of the data subject as a volunteer

- the appointment (or prospective appointment) of the data subject to any office

- the provision (or prospective provision) by the data subject of any service

This exemption therefore exempts the recipient of a reference from the UK GDPR's provisions on:

- the right of a data subject to be informed

- the right of access of a data subject

- all the data protection principles as far as they relate to the right to be informed and the right of access

Inaccurate references

Employers can face a different sort of danger when a former employer gives an overly positive reference to encourage an unsatisfactory employee to leave, or when the employee has negotiated a positive reference as part of a settlement agreement. Theoretically, a new employer could sue a former employer for negligent misstatement if the new employer has suffered loss after relying upon a statement given negligently to its detriment. This principle arises from a well-known Court of Appeal case from 1964 called *Hedley Byrne & Co Ltd v Heller & Partners Ltd*. However, for this claim to succeed, the giver of the reference must be shown to have known the purpose of the reference request and can avoid liability by making a clear disclaimer in the reference refusing to accept responsibility for negligent misstatement (see the 2014 High Court case of *AB v Chief Constable*).

An employer who deliberately gives a false reference with the intention that a new employer will rely on it could also be liable to the new employer for the tortious claim of deceit, whether there is a disclaimer or not.

In practice, it will often be difficult to rely on either type of claim where, for example, there is no clear link between the reference and the damage the new employer sustains. For example, if the new employer were to subsequently find out that an employee once underwent a performance improvement process with a former employer who did not mention it, the new employer would struggle to sue for any losses if the new employee was unsuccessful in their new role, especially where the employee had improved under the PIP or the new role is different.

Chapter 12
Police checks and criminal records

Some roles require the employee to satisfy certain criteria in terms of criminal convictions and offences. If disclosure of this information is necessary for a specific role, the requirement should be made clear in the job advertisements, but the actual vetting should only be carried out in respect of successful candidates.

In England and Wales, an employer may be able to apply to the Disclosure and Barring Service (DBS), and in Scotland to Disclosure Scotland for two types of criminal records information about a prospective employee. A **standard certificate** contains details about a person's:

- spent and unspent convictions

- spent and unspent cautions

- police reprimands and warnings

An **enhanced certificate** contains the same details as a standard certificate, plus:

- 'relevant police information', being any sufficiently serious, current and credible information that a chief officer of a relevant police force reasonably believes to be relevant (having regard to the purpose for which the certificate is requested) and ought to be included.

- where relevant to the post being applied for, any information stored about the person on statutory lists, which contain details of persons who are considered unsuitable to work with children or vulnerable adults.

In order to be permitted to apply for a standard or enhanced check, the role must be listed in the Rehabilitation of Offenders Act 1974 (Exceptions) Order 1975 (the Exceptions Order), and the applying organisation must either register with the DBS (if eligible to do so) to carry out online checks or use an intermediary 'umbrella' body to do so if they are not eligible. Eligibility criteria include being entitled to ask excepted questions under the Exceptions Order, submitting at least 100 applications per year and being able to comply with the requirements of the DBS' code of practice.

The standard or enhanced certificate will first be issued to the individual, who has the right to challenge the content prior to it being released to you, the prospective employer. There are processes in place to challenge the contents and resolve any disputes.

An individual who has subscribed to the DBS' online Update Service, allowing them to take their DBS certificates between jobs, may give an organisation permission to check the database online to see whether any new information has been entered since the last certificate. Criminal record conviction and barring information is updated weekly.

Obviously, an individual candidate can request copies of their own criminal records, such as convictions and cautions, via a data subject access request, but in the vast majority of cases, requiring an individual to obtain them as a condition of employment is a criminal offence under section 184 of the Data Protection Act 2018. An individual, but not an organisation, can also apply to the DBS (if they live in England or Wales) or Disclosure Scotland for a basic certificate showing any unspent convictions and unconditional cautions.

When applying for a standard or enhanced certificate, details of spent convictions will be withheld under the Rehabilitation of Offenders Act 1974 unless the occupation, office or profession is listed in the Exceptions Order. The list of exceptions is too long to replicate here, but they broadly fall into the following categories:

- professions, such as lawyers, accountants and certain medical staff

- certain regulated occupations, such as the financial services industry

- people working with children, providing care services to vulnerable adults and people working in health services

- people who could pose a risk to national security

- people employed to uphold the law

A sample of the periods of rehabilitation in relation to non-exempted roles are currently as follows:

- **never spent:** a custodial sentence over four years or a public protection custodial sentence for specific sexual and violent offences

- **spent after seven years:** a custodial sentence of between two and a half years and four years

- **spent after four years:** a custodial sentence of between six months and two and a half years

- **Spent after two years:** custodial sentences of up to six months

- **Spent after one year:** Fines, community or youth rehabilitation orders

- An absolute discharge is treated as spent immediately

A candidate is not obliged to disclose the detail or existence of any spent convictions, and may not be excluded from office for refusing to do so, unless the role falls within the exemptions, although there is no clear remedy for a candidate who is wrongly excluded, save perhaps by making a complaint to the ICO about their personal data being unlawfully processed. An existing employee who is dismissed on the basis of a spent conviction has the right to bring a claim of unfair dismissal (but not automatic unfair dismissal).

Where a role does fall within an exemption, the candidate must be informed that they are obliged to answer questions about spent convictions.

Where a certificate discloses criminal convictions or cautions up to the date of the certificate, only the basic details of the offence are usually shown, and youth cautions, reprimands and warnings, and multiple convictions are not automatically disclosed. The details may be disclosed in an enhanced certificate where the police deem it relevant to the role the individual intends to work in.

Overseas convictions may also not be disclosed, and you should bear this in mind if you are employing someone who has lived overseas for substantial periods of time, as there may be complexities involved in obtaining such information.

Having received a certificate, you must then decide what to do with the information if any convictions or cautions are disclosed. Where you have discretion (and you will not always, depending on the role in question), you should carry out a risk assessment, including the age of any convictions, their seriousness and their relevance to the role in question.

Data protection considerations

You may only process personal data about an individual's criminal convictions and offences committed under certain situations. These conditions are set out in Parts 1, 2 and 3 of Schedule 1 of the Data Protection Act 2018.

One condition is that the processing must be necessary for the purposes of performing or exercising obligations or rights that are imposed or conferred by law on the controller or data subject in connection with employment.

In addition, there must be an appropriate policy document in place as well as the additional safeguards set out in Part 4 of Schedule 1 of the Data Protection Act 2018. Please see the section on special category personal data in Chapter 4 for more information about the policy document and the additional safeguards.

You may also process personal data about an individual's criminal convictions and offences committed where the employee or candidate has given their express consent, or where one of the substantial public interest conditions set out in Part 2 of Schedule 1 of the Data Protection Act 2018 has been met (provided that an appropriate policy document is in place, along with the additional safeguards set out in Part 4 of Schedule 1).

The substantial public interest conditions are:

- administration of justice

- preventing fraud

- terrorism or money laundering

- race equality

- specific circumstances

Most employers seeking to recruit will rely on the express consent condition before obtaining and processing data about someone's criminal convictions and offences committed.

See the DBS website and the DBS code of practice for guidance on the criminal check regime.

Chapter 13
The contract of employment

The contract of employment is the most important document governing the relationship between employer and employee, although a contract may be wholly or partly oral (often called verbal) as well. However, it is highly recommended to issue all staff with comprehensive writsten contracts of employment that cover all key aspects of the relationship so that there is certainty.

There is, theoretically, an almost infinite number of clauses that could be included in a commercial contract, but contracts of employment are heavily curtailed by statutory requirements and limitations and the personal nature of the service between an employee and an employer. Courts will not usually order a party to do a thing contemplated by an employment contract, although they will restrain parties from doing something that would breach the contract.

It is important that the new employee or worker is given a copy of the contract before they start work, if possible, with enough time for them to review it and raise questions, with the aim that all of the key terms and conditions of employment or engagement are agreed in advance. This is especially important in the case of an employee with significant confidentiality clauses and post-termination restrictive covenants in their contract, as they will not bind the employee unless the covenants are expressly agreed to (and provided they are reasonable).

If, as sometimes happens, a contract is not agreed in advance, you should be able to rely on a custom and practice argument later down the line in relation to terms and conditions, such as pay and benefits and employee duties, as the day-to-day practice will have already been established, and can be proven. However, for terms that relate to less common events and contingencies or are intended to be effective after the employment has ended, such as restrictive covenants, that argument will not work.

Statutory requirement to give information

Restrictive covenants are not mandatory in a contract of employment, but there is a statutory requirement to give both an employee and, since 6 April 2020, a worker, a significant amount of information from day one. A large amount of the information has to be given no later than the first day of employment in a single document. That can be the contract of employment (or the contract for services for a worker), but the information can also be given in a separate document called a principal statement of employment particulars (sometimes called a 'section 1 statement' after section

1 of the Employment Rights Act 1996, where the obligation is set out). The information it must contain is as follows:

- the names of the employer, and the employee or worker

- the date the employment began

- with respect to an employee only, the date their period of continuous employment began

- the scale or rate of pay, or the method of calculating pay

- how often payment will be made

- that the employee or worker has to work on a Sunday, if relevant

- that the employee or worker has to work overtime, if relevant

- terms and conditions relating to:

  ○ hours of work, including normal working hours, the days of the week to be worked and whether they are variable (and if so, in what way)

  ○ holiday entitlement, public holidays and holiday pay

  ○ any other benefits

- the job title or a brief description of the work

- how long the employment is intended to last, and, if it is a fixed-term contract, what the end date is

- any probationary period, including its conditions and duration

- the place of work, or an indication that the employee or worker is required to work at various locations, and the employer's address

Where the employee or worker is required to work outside the United Kingdom for a period of more than one month, you must advise them in the principal statement of:

- the period for which they are to work abroad

- the currency in which remuneration is to be paid

- any additional remuneration and any benefits to be provided as a result of being required to work abroad

- any terms and conditions relating to their return to the UK

Since April 2020, the employer must advise the employee or worker about any training you require them to complete and whether or not you will pay for the training.

You must also give the employee or worker information about the following on day one, but this does not have to be in the principal statement:

- sick leave and sick pay

- any other paid leave

- length of notice of termination the employee must give and is entitled to receive

There is a further set of information that you must give to employees and workers, but which does not have to be given immediately, as long as it is given within two months of the start of the employment. This is information about:

- pensions

- any relevant collective agreements that directly affect the terms and conditions of the employment

- any non-compulsory training the employer requires the employee or worker to complete

- disciplinary and grievance procedures

Employees and workers can also request that you provide an updated statement of particulars , which must be delivered no later than a month after the request has been made.

Be careful if you include some of this information in a contract, rather than a non-contractual separate statement of employment particulars, because you could unwittingly convert a non-contractual benefit into a contractual one.

What if you don't give a statement?

There is no right for employees and workers to bring a claim on its own that they have not been given the information required by section 1 of the Employment Rights Act 1996. However, if an employee or worker wins a separate claim in the ET, they may be awarded an additional two to four weeks' pay if they can prove that they were not provided with a compliant written statement (subject to a statutory cap of £1,142 or £2,284 for the period 6 April 2022 to 5 April 2023). While not a huge sum in itself, it could be multiplied if several members of a large workforce all successfully bring claims as part of other litigation.

A tip is to give workers a differently worded statement from that which you give employees to avoid using language or terminology that could support a claim that a worker was actually an employee.

Data protection information

As explained more fully in Chapter 4, which covers data protection, any organisation that collects and processes personal information about any living individual has to provide information to the data subjects regarding any personal data about them that is being collected and processed. There is no prescribed way to do this, but the most convenient way is to issue a Privacy Notice.

Policies

Any information relating to the management of the relationship needs to be given to employees and workers so that they are fully informed of what is expected of them. Getting them to acknowledge in writing that they have read and understood each policy is strongly recommended to avoid staff denying all knowledge of a requirement or practice later down the line if a disciplinary matter arises.

If staff are dealing in information that is of commercial value to the business, you should expressly draw to their attention the fact that such information is considered to be confidential, of value and subject to the confidentiality obligations that should be in their contracts. This is because a common tactic used by people facing an injunction for misuse of confidential information is to deny that they knew the information was regarded as confidential or of value.

Also by
Daniel Barnett

Available on Amazon
or visit
go.danielbarnett.com/books

IMMEDIATE ACCESS
TO PRAGMATIC & PRACTICAL
HR & EMPLOYMENT LAW ADVICE
YOU CAN
IMMEDIATELY
PUT TO USE FROM
THE **SHARPEST** THOUGHT LEADERS
& HR PROFESSIONALS IN THE UK

FROM THE DESK OF DANIEL BARNETT

August 2022

Dear HR Professional,

You've got so many things going on at work.

The tricky HR issues you have to handle take up your time, your energy and your brain power. It can be exhausting to work under that level of pressure.

Maintaining your high standards of professionalism can be a real struggle, especially when your efforts and expertise often go unappreciated.

You have to make decisions on challenging HR situations you've sometimes never encountered before. Even if you're part of a team, it can feel like you're working in isolation.

With so much complexity and ambiguity, it's not always clear whether you're doing the right thing when there is so much to think about.

It can be draining. You've got to make tough decisions which may be unpopular. You need to ensure people are treated fairly while the business complies with its legal obligations. You've got pressure coming at you from all sides.

Doubt can creep in. What if you've got it wrong? You might even begin to question yourself.

You've got to cope with all that, whilst constantly having to convince any doubting stakeholders you're adding value to the business.

That's where the HR Inner Circle comes in. It's designed to ease that pressure by giving you swift access to resources and practical guidance you can implement right away.

Information I know that saves you time, energy and effort; resources packed full of practical, actionable advice that's difficult to find anywhere else; and a vibrant, active community of caring, like minded HR professionals willing to help you.

It's so easy to find what you want. And it doesn't matter what you're working on.

Whether it be workforce engagement, attracting and keeping talent, diversity and inclusion or employee health and well being, you'll find support for all of that.

You're covered even if you're working on one of those tricky, sensitive, people problems you never see coming until they land squarely on your plate.

Timely Support To Make Your Job Easier, Can Be Rapidly Found In The HR Inner Circle

As a member of the HR Inner Circle, all you have to do is ask. Or just do a quick search in the members' area (more about how easy that is in a moment).

Your first port of call is the vibrant Facebook group, bursting at the seams with incredible HR professionals like you. Just post your question and let it bubble and simmer in the collective genius of the group.

By the end of the day, you'll have at least 3-5 comments on your post, often more. You'll get relevant, insightful and practical guidance that comes from the hard earned experience of your fellow members.

Often you'll get a response within a couple of hours. Sometimes you'll get an answer within minutes - even if it's late in the evening!

This highly active community never fails to astound with just how willing they are to help fellow HR professionals like you by sharing their knowledge and experience.

While you wait for your answer from the Facebook group, you can also search the members' vault in our secure online portal. It takes just 2 clicks and a quick keyword search using our Rapid Results Search Tool.

Instantly, you'll find exactly where your topic is covered in our extensive back catalogue of monthly magazines and audio seminars. One more click and you're straight there. In under 30 seconds you can find exactly what you're after. It's that quick and easy.

If you need a specific legal insight, pose your question live to an expert employment lawyer in our monthly Q&A session.

It'll either be me or one of my prominent contemporaries. Get your answer immediately without having to pay any legal costs.

A quick search of the previous Q&A sessions, and you'll find where it's been answered before. Our clever index system means you can find a question, and in one click get straight to the answer.

But perhaps you need to dive deep and explore the different options open to you?

Then join one of our monthly HR Huddles. There you can run your specific situation past other HR professionals. They'll offer their insights, share their experience and work WITH you to find a solution that works FOR you.

It's A Labour Of Love Putting All This Together For You.

I've spent years practising law and have become recognised as one of the UK's leading employment law barristers. I've even got my own radio show! But more importantly for you, I've also developed another skill.

It's bringing employment expertise AND practical experience together in a way that supports busy, overworked (and sometimes stressed) HR professionals like you.

Being a member now means your business and clients will see you as even more informed about the intricacies of employment law. They'll marvel at how well you keep up to date when you're so busy working hard for them.

You'll be seen making quicker decisions and implementing solutions that will accelerate the growth of the organisation. You'll make impressive time and cost savings for the business.

And those tricky, off-piste situations you've never come across before? Well, nothing will faze you, because you're backed up by an HR support system second to none.

But more importantly, you'll feel that pressure gently ease off.

That's Why I'm Inviting You To Reap The Many Rewards Of Membership

Here's what you get when you join the HR Inner Circle:

 Firstly, you'll get unlimited access to the hugely popular HR Inner Circle Facebook Private Group (Value: £1,188.00 a year)

- Tap into the vast wealth of knowledge, experience, insight and wisdom of the top 0.5% of your profession at any time, day or night.

- In less than 5 minutes you can post ANY HR question and get insightful answers and suggestions in a couple of hours or less, from some of the best in your profession.

- Fast track your impact by discovering effective shortcuts and workarounds from people who've been "there" and done "it".

- Expand and deepen your network of like minded individuals, secure in the knowledge they're as dedicated and as ambitious as you.

- Increase your prestige with your colleagues and stakeholders by being part of such an exclusive and prominent HR community.

- Gain confidence in your judgment and decisions by using the highly responsive community as a sounding board for your ideas.

"The HR Inner Circle is fantastic support for HR Professionals. The Facebook group is a great sense check when you work on your own and a great way to get a different perspective.."

Nancy Prest, HR Professional

"The HR Inner Circle is the best CPD investment you can make. Regardless of how you learn best, there is something for everyone and you're always up to date about employment law, case law and the subtle gray areas in between. If it's not already written down, just ask the group and someone will have the answer."

Lara Kenny, HR Professional

"The HR Inner Circle is an extremely helpful forum in which to bounce around ideas with very knowledgeable and experienced HR professionals and ask for advice and views on employment relations issues."

Yolaine Bech, HR Professional

2 Secondly, you'll receive 11 copies of the HR Inner Circular Magazine every year (Value: £350.00 annual subscription)

- Enjoy that satisfying "THUD" on your door mat every month when the postman delivers your very own copy of the HR Inner Circular magazine.

- Quickly discover exactly what the law says about key issues affecting HR professionals around the UK who are just like you.

- Get concise and practical guidance on how employment law applies to the challenging situations and circumstances you deal with every day.

- Avoid the mistakes of others by applying the lessons from the in depth analysis of real life case studies.

- Benefit from a legal deep dive by the UK's leading employment law barrister into a topical employment question posed by a fellow member (perhaps you!).

- Review a summary of recent important Facebook Group discussions worthy of sharing, that you may have missed.

- Learn from a range of related and relevant topics useful for your practice and your broader professional development.

"I thoroughly recommend the HR Inner Circle. It's worth every penny from the monthly magazine to the weekly podcast to the monthly audio seminars. And just having the support network to call on for a comfort blanket from time to time. I've been a member since it started"

Alison Melville, HR Professional

3 Thirdly, you get an exclusive invite to a live online Q&A Session every month, led by an expert employment lawyer (Value: £199.00 a session or £2,388 a year)

- Gain 60 minutes of live and direct access to the sharpest legal minds from my secret little black book of contacts.

- Get answers to your knottiest employment law questions, and solutions to your trickiest HR problems, from some of the brightest employment lawyers in the UK.

- Avoid having to pay the £300-£400 it would cost you to ask a lawyer your question outside of the HR Inner Circle.

- Benefit from valuable insights from the answers given to other members.

- If you can't attend live, watch the recording when it's convenient for you.

- Quickly access the recorded answer to any question asked in the session by simply clicking the question index for that session.

- Save time by downloading the session transcription to scan-read at a time suitable for you.

> *"The HR Inner Circle gives you access to Daniel's practical and straightforward advice on employment issues. The businesses I work with don't want jargon, they just want pragmatic advice and I can access that through HR Inner Circle"*
>
> *Mandy Carr, HR Professional*
>
> *"It's a breath of fresh air to have an HR resource which gives practical advice and tips. We can find out the law but it's the application of the law and HR practice led by a barrister along with the opinions of other HR professionals in the Q&A sessions which are invaluable"*
>
> *Caroline Robertson, HR Professional*

 **Fourthly, Join a live Monthly Huddle with other HR Professionals to solve your most challenging HR problems
(Value: £1,188.00 a year)**

- Attend your very own mini-mastermind group of highly qualified, highly regarded and experienced fellow HR professionals to "group think" through an issue you're facing right now.

- Develop bespoke solutions to the unique problems and challenges you have to deal with in a safe, supportive and confidential environment.

- Feel safe knowing these online zoom calls are NOT recorded to respect the sensitivity of issues addressed and the privacy of those involved. [NOTE - a professional transcriber attends and takes written notes. An anonymised summary is then made available to the membership]

- Recent Huddle topics included changing employee benefits, mandatory vaccination, career breaks, sickness during disciplinaries, effective worker forums and hybrid working arrangements.

"The HR Inner Circle is a great network opportunity to get practical and refreshing approaches for day to day HR and employment law matters. It's great to see that we all experience tricky cases from time to time"

Annabel Carey, HR Professional

"HR can be a lonely role and as the person advising everyone around you, it can often be difficult to find advice and peer support for you as an individual. We all know there are rarely right and wrong answers in HR. It's an art not a science and the HR Inner Circle gives you a group of like minded individuals to share solutions, provide expertise and insight, and a place to go when you just don't have the answers. "

Jo Mosley, HR Professional

5 And finally, Your Personal Concierge will help you get the best out of your membership (Value: Priceless!)

- You get personal access to a personal concierge who'll point you in the direction of exactly where to find what you need. She's supported hundreds of members over the years she's been at my side.

- She also works closely with the 11 back office staff that support the operation. In the extremely unlikely event she doesn't know where something is, she knows who will.

"The Inner Circle is a forum where you can get HR advice in all different formats. The monthly magazines and the audio seminars, the Facebook group and the annual conference. It is excellent value for money."

Christine Cooper, HR Professional

"Just join. The resources available to the HR Inner Circle members are invaluable especially the Facebook group where you can get advice or a different point of view that you may not have previously considered outside of normal working hours which is really useful. Live Q&As too."

Diana Wilks, HR Professional

How Much Does joining the HR Inner Circle Cost?

Let me remind you of the annual value of membership you get when you join:

Access to the private Facebook Group	£ 1,188.00
HR Inner Circular Magazine subscription	£ 350.00
Live Q&A sessions	£ 2,388.00
Monthly HR Huddles	£ 1,188.00
Your Personal Membership Concierge	PRICELESS!

TOTAL £ 5,114.00

But you're not going to pay anywhere near that. **All it's going to cost you is just £96 +VAT per month. That's the equivalent of the price of a daily Starbucks.**

Another way of looking at your investment is this:

It's like having your very own part time, legally trained, assistant HR Business Partner, just waiting to provide you with all the answers you need…. **all for just £96+VAT per month.**

And that price is fixed for as long as you remain a member.

Plus, With Membership Of The HR Inner Circle, You'll Also Get These 6 Bonuses Worth £3,305.00 For FREE!

Bonus #1: Free Access To The Annual Conference every May (Value: £399)

The perfect opportunity to extend your personal network and gather key insights and takeaways to help you personally and professionally. Includes lunch too.

Bonus #2 - Monthly Audio Seminars (Value: £588.00)

A 60 minute legal deep dive by me into an important subject relevant to you and your practice every month (downloadable mp3).

Bonus #3 - Handling Awkward Conversations (Value: £997.00)

A video case study masterclass you can share with managers to train them to handle awkward staff disciplinary, performance and attitude problems.

Bonus #4 - 4 x HR Employment Online Courses (Value: £388.00)

Deconstructing TUPE, Changing Terms & Conditions, Unconscious Bias At Work and Handling Grievances.

Bonus #5 - Free listing on the Register of Investigators (Value: £250.00)

Advertise your professional investigations service in our member's portal

Bonus #6 - Significant Discounts On My Flagship Products (Value: £683.00)

Get member discounts on my Getting Redundancy Right and HR Policies products as well as other price reductions as new products are released.

I'm So Confident Joining The HR Inner Circle Is The Right Decision For You, Here's My 100% Satisfaction "Buy It Back" Guarantee

Take action and join the HR Inner Circle now. If you're not 100% satisfied with your investment after 30 days, I'll refund and buy EVERYTHING back from you.

I'm comfortable doing this because I know once you join, you'll find the support, the information and the strategies so useful, you'll never want to leave.

Before you decide though, let me be very clear about membership of the HR Inner Circle.

It's only for ambitious and dedicated HR professionals who want to accelerate and increase their impact by plugging into an HR ecosystem with its finger firmly on the pulse of what's working right now in HR. If you're just plodding along and are content with just getting by, then this is probably not for you.

But if you're drawn to benefiting from standing shoulder to shoulder with some of the giants in the HR community, then re-joining the HR Inner Circle is the RIGHT decision for you. Join here now:

www.hrinnercircle.co.uk

Daniel Barnett

PS after you join www.hrinnercircle.co.uk, if you don't feel it's right for you, we'll refund anything you've paid if you ask within 30 days.

If you are looking for a forum to discuss confidential issues that need prompt employment law advice, then the HR Inner Circle is definitely for you. In addition it offers other tools to help and support. The Facebook group is full of information and solutions to scenarios — invaluable for HR professionals.

- Sheena Doyle, Managing Director, The Really Useful HR Company Ltd

It's a forum where you're not afraid to ask stupid questions, even though I'm not usually afraid of doing that. The sheer variety of experience and skillsets ensures there is always an informed discussion. JOIN NOW!!

- Jon Dews, HR & Business Partner, Majestic 12 Ltd

If you are looking for a steady stream of thorough, pragmatic, and easily-digestible employment law advice, the HR Inner Circle is a great place to be.

- Susi O'Brien, Senior Manager HR, The Action Group

The regular updates are invaluable to not only me, but also my team. We find that they are presented in an easy to digest format and aren't too 'legalistic'.

- Donna Negus, Sekoya Specialist Employment Services

WWW.HRINNERCIRCLE.CO.UK

There aren't many other employment law advice services where you get direct access to an employment law barrister at a realistic price. Join the HR Inner Circle now – you won't regret it.

- **Kirsten Cluer**, Owner of Cluer HR, HR Consultancy

I like being able to use the HR Inner Circle Facebook group to ask other members for a second opinion, or for ideas when I get stuck with solving a tricky situation. There's usually someone who has come across the situation before.

- **Helen Astill**, Managing Director, Cherington HR Ltd

When I transitioned from big employers to an SME, I didn't realise how much I would miss having peers to kick ideas around. If you haven't got an internal network, you've got to build an external one. I got so much out of the discussion at an Inner Circle meetup recently and I look forward to getting the Inner Circular.

- **Elizabeth Divver**, Group HR Director, The Big Issue Group

Sign now! The monthly Q & A sessions are invaluable, the magazine is packed full of helpful info, you get lots of goodies and the Facebook page is really informative and a useful sounding board.

- **Caroline Hitchen**, Consultant, Caroline Neal Employment Law

WWW.HRINNERCIRCLE.CO.UK

Being a member of HR Inner Circle is one of the best sources of HR information and advice, and receiving the monthly audio seminars and magazines is extremely helpful and interesting. I can't recommend becoming a member highly enough. There is a private Facebook group which is great for asking other members advice and sharing knowledge and experiences. I have also recently attended one of the meetups that is organised by Daniel Barnett, and it was good to meet other members (and of course Daniel) in a more social setting. It was also a good opportunity to ask any questions you wanted and being able to get advice or support as to how they would deal with whatever you ask.

- **Tracey Seymour**, HR Manager (Head of Dept), Kumon Europe & Africa Ltd

The help and advice from other HR professionals on Facebook is really valuable, and quick. All the team enjoy the audio seminars and magazines for updates on current issues.

- **Catherine Larke**, Director | myHRdept.co.uk

For me it's a no brainer. We have a lot of really good contributors in the HR Inner Circle and it's more than a discussion forum and invaluable source of information. When combined with the magazine, the audio seminars and events, it is a complete service especially with Daniel's legal expertise always on hand.

- Elizabeth Ince, Self employed HR Consultant

Just join! It is invaluable with the resources you have at hand by joining the HR Inner Circle. Especially the Facebook Group where you can get advice or a different point of view that you may not have previously considered, outside of normal working hours which is very useful. Live Q&A's too.

- Diana Wilks, HR Manager, Go South Coast Ltd

HR can be complex because each and every issue will have its own set of individual circumstances. Being in the HR Inner Circle enables you to bounce ideas around and make sure you are considering every angle and aspect, knowing your HR Inner Circle partners will have had a similar experience to share.

- Pam Rogerson, HR Director, ELAS Group

WWW.HRINNERCIRCLE.CO.UK

**Use your time wisely.
Let us help.**

Regain your freedom and focus on running your business.

FeMan Consulting offers HR support, advice and guidance.

⊕ www.femanconsulting.co.uk   ✉ mike@femanconsulting.co.uk